ANCHOR BOOKS

LADIES OF TELEVISION

First published in Great Britain in 1993 by
ANCHOR BOOKS
1-2 Wainman Road, Woodston,
Peterborough, PE2 7BU

Foreword

Anchor Books is a small press, established in 1992, with the aim of promoting readable poetry to as wide an audience as possible.

We hope to establish an outlet for writers of poetry who may have struggled to see their work in print.

Following our request in the National Press, we were overwhelmed by the response. The poems presented here have been selected from many entries. Editing proved to be a difficult and daunting task and as the Editor, the final selection was mine.

The poems chosen represent a cross-section of styles and content. They have been sent from all over the country, written by young and old alike, united in the passion for writing poetry.

I trust this selection will delight and please the authors and all those who enjoy reading poetry.

Michelle Abbott
Editor

Contents

The Famous Housewife

She's eight foot two with hair of blue
Does this sound like a Martian to you?
She's famous world-wide
She's acted, painted and once been in prison
But emerges unscathed from whatever's arisen
Her antics are limited only by the imagination
Yet she's never considered a source of fascination
She's more human than you or I
She's the perfect mother who makes pumpkin pie
She's the family fount of good sense and affection
Though they sometimes stray from the right direction!
Though she may not pursue the American Dream
She believes in the family and hers are a team!
She's content with neither accolade nor wealth
She takes greater pride in her family's health
What woman wouldn't understand
Love to meet her and shake her hand?
For this same woman has often made history
But if her identity is still a mystery . . .
There isn't an actress in the world who could play her
Because she's Marge Simpson
Only the pencil can ever portray her!

Emma Berens

Keeping Up Appearances

Hyacinth's terribly busy today,
She is rushing madly in every direction,
For a candlelight supper is on the way
And her parties must never be less than perfection.
Poor Richard is rubbing the silver up bright,
The hand-painted china is out on display.
It will glow in the shimmering candle light
Arranged in Hyacinth's inimitable way.

After the supper she sometimes sings:
The man next door is fearfully certain
She'll ask him to play: when his door bell rings
Trembling, he cowers behind a curtain.
His sister, Liz, would help and is able,
But whenever she enters Hyacinth's house
She drops the cups, leaves crumbs on the table,
And is paralysed as a frightened mouse.

In mid preparation there comes a slight scare:
It is Sheridan 'phoning to speak to his Mummy.
He wants silk pyjamas, like his friends wear,
And for these he will need some extra money.
Hyacinth's eyebrows go up, but she smiles;
Yes, Richard will put a big cheque in the post.
The boy must keep up with the latest styles,
For appearances always count the most.

Hyacinth's *dos* are a social *must*:
On the way up quite a stepping stool:
For she only invites the Upper Crust,
Like those with two baths and a swimming pool.
The guests arrive - all is set to impress,
And the candlelight supper's a huge success,

Eileen Morgan

A Poem for a Celebrity

She has ginger hair
And a great big smile
When on the TV she dresses with style,
She sings and she jokes
Whilst hosting her shows,
And leaves tears of joy wherever she goes,
Arranging *Blind Dates*
Excitement rises,
Or she is engaged springing surprises,
She's had her name changed,
From white - now to black,
And she's never short of a witty wise-crack,
She's a *lorra* fun
A real *spine-chiller*
My favourite personality,
Cilla Cilla Cilla.

L M Bird

Sue Pollard

Is a character I'll ner'e forget.
Standing at the stage door we met
'Hello!' I said 'Have you come to audition?'
'Yes! To sing on stage is my ambition.'
'I too,' I said 'have come to have a go.'
'Let's go in,' says Sue. 'They can only say yes or no.'
'Who's this then Peggy?' the producer said.
'Her name is Sue, she's come to sing for you.'
'Right,' says he, 'go to the pianist and sing this song.'
'A lovely voice,' the producer said, 'she'll do.'
So in *The Student Prince* a lead part
As Kathie she got her start.
But now our Sue is a star
On TV I see her from afar.
She's made her name as a comedienne
Don't suppose I'll ever meet this character again.

Peggy Schofield

Who Came to my House?

My door was open, my *Heart Beat* fast,
I entered my hall, did I disturb the raiders?
Was this a case for Miss Marple or Morse?
Or could *The Bill* tackle *The Invaders*?

Was it that ice-man, nice-man, David Frost
And Loyd *Through the Keyhole* looking and spying?
Or the smiling, bearded David Bellamy
Under the floorboards, poking and prying?

Sounds from the kitchen - Delia Smith?
Or *Master Chef*? Take a quick scan -
Chopsticks, stir-fry, Chinese delights -
Someone can cook - it must be Yan!

Into the lounge now, the trail's hotting up,
But I open the door and I gasp and pant -
Is it *Noel's House Party*? The room is full,
All my relations - and my long lost Aunt!

Well it wasn't David, Loyd, Delia or Yan
Who invaded my humble suburban villa,
Who brought all my relatives in by the score -
Surprise! Surprise! It was our luvly Cilla!

Rhona Mitchell

Jim Versus Liz

Jim had been fine in the Army days
He was the man of the house.
But now those days were over,
Had he become Man or Mouse!
He no longer felt he had family
To support, and keep safe and sound -
Andy, away at his college
While Steve his own life had found.
But the thing that made life so sad -
Was the fact his wife Liz had gone too.
Manageress of a Pub if you please
What had he got? and who?
The only place Jim felt at home,
Was propping up the bar!
He wasn't concerned with the life around.
Had things now gone too far?
Liz knocked on the door one morning
Jim, asked why she'd used no key
'I didn't think I had the right!
Now this is not home to me.'
She politely asked how his Father was -
Knowing him to be ill -
'He's picking up nicely now,' Jim replied,
'My dad has a very strong will.'
Liz hurried towards the door to go,
But beforehand, gave Jim a brief kiss.
He sat in the chair, his head in his hands
Did he have to live like this.
He missed his sons, he missed his wife
Alone, in the house, day and night.
He'd just go on hoping for Liz to come back
And together again, love and happiness bright.

Rosemarie Wood-Hall

Thora Hird

There is something we look forward to
Sunday evening after tea,
time to pull up the armchair
there's a friend we have to see.

She has a touch of cosy humour
which cheers if life is full of gloom
just get up and turn the switch
to have her right there in the room.

It's that special sincerity
seen on her sunny face
and when your heart is heavy
puts it right back in its place.

The chosen hymns are so uplifting
bringing our Lord's presence ever new
in those healing words we feel his strength
when we sing along with you.

In this sad and often thoughtless world
we need her comforting honesty
so for the joy of Thora Hird
I have to say, 'Praise Be.'

G Price

To Joely Richardson

When cowed by someone, as when being interviewed
We are told to imagine them completely nude
This is to degrade them in the mind's eye,
To reduce them to the level of you and I.
Yet now programme makers show us stars in the buff
More nakedness, more sex, surely *nuff is enuff?*
Sex used to be called making love, and kept private too
A sacred thing between two people - not put on view.
Clothes maketh man we've always been told
They enhance people, as well as keep out the cold!

Dear Joely Richardson, you were so sweet and pure
We're forced now to accept you as far from demure
From now on you will be the subject of jest,
Of lewd remarks, and *that was the girl who undressed*
Did you hear of viewers who turned on for the sport,
Not really wanting the dull story - just the cavort
Nothing left to the imagination - there you were -
Making us all into an excited voyeur
There's videos for those who need titillation
Why not keep more mystique and intrigue for the nation?

Midge Clarke

Anneka Rice

Anneka Rice
Is very nice -
So very energetic;
Such splendid zeal,
One has to feel,
Is probably genetic.

Her teeth so bright -
So dazzling white,
You need to wear your goggles;
And then, for some,
Her shapely bum -
Imagination boggles.

But if you think
That cheeky wink,
(So sexy and appealing),
Is meant for you,
It isn't true! -

But who, we're not revealing.

Margot Cowlin

Our Cilla

Our Cilla is a Liverpool lass,
Her shows are great, a real touch of class.
The colour of her hair, is what might be called red
('It's from a bottle' she tells us all)
And Cilla would give a chirpy
'Surprise Surprise,' if she came knocking at your door.

Our Cilla is able to take control,
When brash blind daters come on the show.
Her Liverpool humour comes out thick and fast,
(When contestants try to be smug,)
But our Cilla's too quick, she's right on the ball,
And ends up having the last laugh!

Our Cilla brings people together,
She also makes wishes come true,
She's vibrant and fun,
She's my Number One,
And surprise surprise I bet she's yours too!

Elizabeth Roberts

Hyacinth

Hyacinth's no wilting wallflower.
She's always frightened at what the
neighbours might see as curtains
on her tree lined avenue twitch threateningly.
High tea is partaken with due deference.
Her voice shrill as a dentist's
drill pipes up 'Did you hear my
dear terrible shame.' 'Yes Jeremy
caught cooking the books what an
example for the working classes.'
With Hyacinth this is what
passes for polite conversation
leaving everyone feeling mentally
plundered as if after an interrogation.
It's living among the lower middle
classes that does it.
But aspiring to act with upper class affectation.
Leaving a trail of resentment
in her wake on her tree lined
avenue as curtains twitch threateningly.

Barbara McLoughlin

TV Personality

The television personality most prominent in mind,
Is the one that brings together she thinks are two of a kind,
Her show is entertaining with a varied spark,
Her guests are people who sometimes leave their mark.
She is unusual in this show quest,
Not one you see, but three at a time her varied guests
Hoping to find a boy or girlfriend to partner for life,
Sometimes young or middle aged for a husband or wife,
This Northern Television Personality
Hosts not one show, but two.
She is wonderful in giving a surprise surprise
That could be for you,
She is fashionable and popular, good looking and fair,
She sings songs of affection and tells of her care,
She brings folks together, from far and near
Families or friends lost from yester year.
But still she holds dear, close to her heart we all know
The closeness of her family to love and grow.
I bet you have guessed, *It's Cilla Black* you see!
Because we all love her personality.

Muriel A Taylor

Unexpurgated

On Sunday evenings, latterly,
Absorbed with Lady Chatterly,
I realised, when it left the screen,
I knew the meaning of *has been*.

C Foster

Last of the Summer Love

How I love you, Norah Batty
How I love your wrinkled tights,
They're in my thoughts, each waking hour,
And in my dreams, at night,

To brave the steps up to your door,
Wells up in me a fire,
And when you hit me with your broom,
It fills me with desire,

For you I'd have a bath each month,
If it would gain me merit,
And just to have my love returned,
I'd even sell me ferret.

We'll have a lovely wedding,
Some sandwiches and jellies.
You in your posh wedding gown,
And me in my washed wellies.

You are my Yorkshire Juliet,
So tell me please, en-prompto
If I can be your Romeo.
From your ever loving Compo.

Jennifer Allanson

Birds of a Feather

Dorien, oh Dorien what a joy to behold
As you trip next door to the prisoner's wives
You just cannot leave alone.

They've brought disgrace to Chigwell
You know this very well,
But it's all so exciting
And someone else to tell
Your latest exploits with men!

You can't help being nosy
It's all part of your charm,
And so ready with your good advice
To Tracy's - but rarely Sharon's - latest tale of woe.

We know you're very knowledgeable
In many ways than one.
Still you can't help your flirtations
Even if it brings on palpitations
When you think - Marcus might find out!

With painted lips and painted nails
Impeccably dressed - for awhile -
You're really out to trap
The most susceptible of males.

It really was funny
And gave us all a treat,
To see you singing - *Like a Virgin*?
Then being swept right off your feet!

I do not need repeats
To heighten my perception
But in this particular scene I've mentioned
I wait, in anticipation
For the repeat!

V L Brooks

Hyacinth Bucket

Daisy, Hyacinth, Violet, Rose.
Who's the one that everyone knows?
All shiver and shake when she's about.
Boy! Has Hyacinth got some clout!
Milkmen, postmen, creep up her path,
Horribly afraid of *Bucket* wrath.
(Hyacinth would naturally say,
Enlightened people say, 'Bouquet'.)
Next door neighbours have their share,
Poor Emmett's in a cold despair,
Nervous of Hyacinth's piercing trill,
Which really makes him feel quite ill.
Elizabeth dreads words *Coffee Break*,
Deep worrying breaths she'll take,
But she always has a spill.
Hyacinth winces; gives looks to kill.
She lords it over family also,
Although she rarely worries Onslo,
Who won't drop dead from undue stress,
Living in a permanent mess,
With chubby Daisy and flighty Rose,
(Hyacinth keeps them on their toes.)
But Onslo's dog is Hyacinth's boss,
His frenzied barking makes her cross.
The whole household lets her down,
They make Hyacinth fuss and frown,
Save Richard, who does as he's told,
Because he isn't very bold.
Poor Richard, dressed in best big and tucker,
When will he get his *Candlelight Supper*?

Nesta Wilson

A Brush With Nora Batty

Compo's love is plain to see.
Behind his clothes so tatty.
His loving heart is way above
With houseproud Nora Batty.

I think Nora's playing hard to get.
And flaunts her legs to trap him
A little more above the knee.
And she would surely zap him

Foggy and Clegg can't understand
Compo's relentless passion
For a woman who in smiler's words
Took stockings out of fashion.

She wouldn't mind him round her house
This old ungroomed old codger.
But perish the thought of marital bliss
With a ferret as a lodger.

Brian Barton

Cilla Black

I am Miss Cilla from Liverpool
And always trying to please,
The TV audience with my shows
And wobbling at the knees.

Blind Date brings couples together
No matter what the weather,
They try their best and we do the rest
To make this the greatest show ever.

D M Springings

Hyacinth Bucket

Mrs Bucket, that's her name
She drives everyone she knows insane.
They say she's fat and that she's posh.
And of course has lots of dosh.
They think she is so very rich.
But they say she's a bossy witch.
It's her husband I feel sorry for.
She's turned him into a frightful bore.
Whenever she goes into the house.
He feels just like a tiny mouse.
We just told you about Hyacinth Bucket.
The woman people hide from every day.

Nina Biddiss

Penelope Keith

Of all the dames in vanity fair,
I met a dame with golden hair
She was the sweetest you could meet,
There's cupid in her hands and feet.
And she's not married, glad to tell
Tonight I'll meet her at the *Belle*.
But I'm a poor man, and faint hearted,
Before we're married, we'll be parted.
For on a rich man's heart she's bent
Which providence has not yet sent.

Peter Buss

It's She

She's fair, she's plump, she really is good
Her name, I think, sounds something like Wood.
She works at the Acorn
With antiques to sell
How much is sold, I really can't tell.
She and her mates, they talk, over tea
And discuss with each other
What they'd like to be.
She tells them the story
Of her one big swim
The sad part is, she had to give in.
When she plays and sings ditties
You just have to smile
To listen to her
Is really worthwhile.
Her name is Victoria
The greatest by far
Victoria Wood you sure are a star.

R Mitchell

Cilla Black

Anyone who had a heart,
Was all I used to sing,
I'd sing it in the Cilla style,
It was a regular thing,
Then Cilla, she got married,
Children? Three she had,
I got married too and had a girl and a lad.
Our children have grown up now,
And Cilla still keeps on,
Giving us a lorra laughs
and a lorra, lorra fun.
My Daughter has taken over now,
And every Sunday night,
She fills our house with Cilla's theme,
Surprise, surprise tonight.
I reach for the tissues, yes
there's another wonderful deed,
Wouldn't it be lovely Cilla if all the world could heed,
Surprise one another
and put peace throughout the land,
Anyone who had a heart would always lend a hand.

Barbara Hale

A Star

A well known lady fair of face,
Well loved by the human race,
Yet played a part not loved by all,
Which belied her truest self,
A part of avarice and stealth
Of strength and weakness I recall.

She's gone now this many a year,
Yet memory of her is still clear,
In many a heart she lives on still,
In mine a special day of pleasure
A day that I shall always treasure,
She gave to us of her own free will.

She died. She's now at rest.
She lived. Gave always of her best.
I spent a day with her in style
When she opened for us an Animal Home,
Travelling miles with great aplomb,
Her radiance shone there for a while.

A generous soul, she gave so well.
A shining star that never fell.
Except to death's relentless grip.
Who was this lady who dreamed a dream?
Of animals to be held in great esteem,
Why Elsie Tanner of Coronation Street.
or (Pat Phoenix).

S Hardy

The Loveable Landlady!

She manages the bar in a world famous street
It is based on the corner where neighbours all meet.
She greets all her customers with a big cheerful smile
She also looks glamorous and dresses with style.

I will reveal who it is if you have not guessed yet
Her last name is Gilroy, her first is Bet!
She has always been there with a shoulder to cry on
Rita needed her recently when Ted had gone.

At first she worked for Annie, with Fred behind the bar.
Remember that episode with Bet stuck in his car?
Now there are Jack, Betty and Raquel too.
Bet has her hands full, we know this is true!

Dizzy Raquel lodges upstairs in Bet's pub.
Betty cooks hotpot and other tasty grub!
Jack takes care of the work in the cellar.
Always out to make a few bob is this funny fella!

Bet's husband Alec used to run the place
Until he left taking his packed up suitcase
Bet did not want to go with him and leave her friends.
Her head she kept, a broken heart she now mends.

She runs the Rovers Return with such ease
When the clock strikes, she calls 'Time Gentlemen please!'
Young Vicky stays with Bet quite a bit
She still sees Steve though, Alec would have a fit!

Bet is really quite witty amongst other things.
For example she is famous for those large earrings!
She is everything a landlady should be
To see for yourself consult *what's on TV!*

Sharon Varley

Cilla Black

Cilla really made her name,
with songs that also brought her fame.
And programmes like *Surprise Surprise*
Brought lots of tears to everyone's eyes.
She made, people happy attending *Blind Date*,
Their futures were sealed and their celebrate,
Good luck to you Cilla, there's no one like you,
You have made us all happy instead of being blue.

Margaret Miller

Pauline Fowler

Pauline's going out for the day
hopefully to get out of Arthur's way,
Where is she going, we don't know?
but she's taken off her old cardigan and away she goes.
Into the taxi, far and wide
to get away, probably to the seaside.
Round and round Albert Square the taxi goes,
Where's Pauline going, we don't know?
The taxi stops outside the cafe
Pauline stands to chat and laugh
Inside the cafe, she drinks and eats
here comes Michelle, let's beat a hasty retreat,
Back in the taxi, she's on her way
she's happy to be out for the day
She say's to the driver, I know what I'll do
Let's take off this sunny day, off to the zoo.
Back in the taxi, she changes her mind,
but the driver doesn't care, he is kind.
Pauline changes her mind again,
and now it looks like it might rain.
Pauline says let's go down to Albert Square
down to the allotments to find Arthur there.
Then on we go to the Queen Vic
where Sharon says, 'Everyone drink up quick.'
Then on to the launderette to find Dot Cotton
Where shall we go then, I've forgotten?
Back home she sits down, she is so tired
Arthur asks how much was the taxi, she hired.
One day soon, she knows not when, but off she'll go far and wide,
Maybe to Albert Square or the seaside.

J M Stoles

Sharon

My name is Sharon, the landlady of the Queen Vic I am
There's me and there's Grant and he's my old man,
I like to wear short skirts and low cut tops
But that's understandable, after all I was Sharon Watts.
I'm married to Grant but also like Phil quite a bit
'Aving these two blokes around is what makes me tick,
That and being the landlady of the Queen Vic pub
It's a great place to booze and we do quite good grub.

D Oakley

Sister Duffy - Casualty

Doctor doctor doctor Brown,
Comes around to all his patients.
Are you better are you worse,
Oh said the doctor where's your nurse.

In comes Duffy with a red hot poultice,
Dabs it on and takes no notice.
Oh! said the patient that's too hot,
Oh! said Duffy I'm sure it's not.

Then she looked at Mrs Regal,
She had to give her the needle.
She shot it up her bum so high,
The poor woman let out a cry.

You silly nurse what have you done,
You should have taken blood from my thumb.
Sorry dear said Duffy I had to do that too,
Soon you'll feel better after going to the loo.

Duffy was rushing to get away,
Because it was the end of her day.
Then a patient fell out of bed,
Shouting nurse nurse I've hurt my head.

Duffy tried to lift her up,
But the sixteen stone was too much.
Help rushed through the door,
And lifted the woman off the floor.

Duffy said it's not my day,
Believe me we earn our pay.
When I get home my friends will say,
Well have you had a busy day.

M Mitchell

Cilla Black

Surprise, Surprise, what do we have here?
Never fear, ar' Cilla's here.
She'll cheer you up when you are low
Invite you all to watch her show.
She's cheerful and zany though
Black is her name,
Her caring and sharing have brought
Her much fame.
Tears and laughter she's brought to many
The TV licence is worth every penny,
When our Cilla Black graces the screen
There's never a show that's better seen.
With a lorra laughs and a youthful zest
She really is the very best.

Liz Simons

Mrs Chatterley

Give me the life of Lady C:
diaphanous frocks, delicate tea
in spacious still, minimal grime . . .
not this third-rate pantomime
of fetid nappies, fungus, debt,
alien videos, familiar regret.

Make me her gold, a mythic fawn
gambolling on eternal lawn,
under clean sky, amber sun,
listening for the phallic gun
of my poetically common paramour.
I'd relish the role of genteel whore -

Even though my wood's a public park
where dog-piddle dominates the bark
and the keeper's an arthritic OAP
who prefers his local to the BBC,
has a luminous head, a sumo gut,
heats only baked beans in his hut.

I crave her rich man - if not his spleen -
a saviour dangerous as Sean Bean
who'll chase me, starkers, in the rain,
transform wild flowers, sacks of grain,
speak gravel-coarse but act heroic,
draw the wanton from this stoic.

Her title's real whereas I'm Queen of Dust,
have no spare moments to stoke my lust,
be wistful, wilting, sigh out plot,
forget my duty, the cooking-pot,
the ironing-board, the petty slights . . .
Damn! Ken Russell for Sunday nights.

Diane Haslam

She

She never moves or speaks or sings
At sums a seeming dance,
Yet constant over many things
Her smile you know at once,
That girl on Test Card BB2
The female Peter Pan
Unageing, unlike me and you
Has this undying fan.
I met her first in black and white
Then coloured she became,
I recognise her at first sight
Yet never know her name.

D H Johnson

Untitled

Cilla is a wonderful gal
She makes everyone feel like her pal,
On *Blind Date* she will cause a laugh
And for many a couple she has paved the path,
To romance love marriage and bliss
All sealed with a *Blind Date* kiss.
Surprise Surprise warms your heart
To see people come together that's been so long apart,
I think this show is a marvellous thing
And I like to hear Cilla sing.

Winifred McAllister

Thora Hird

All, glory be to Thora Hird
Who makes me sing, just like a bird,
Each Sunday night, when she is seen,
On the Holy, Holy screen.

The light that shines from her dear eyes
Helps us all, to realise
That in this world there's still some good,
And we should help her, if we could.

Now later, as the evening folds,
What, is this, I do behold.
Oh goody goody, it is fine,
There's Thora in *The Summer Wine!*

Sing praises to this lovely lady,
Who thrills us all, though over eighty,
To heaven would soar, our Holy word,
If we were all like *Thora Hird.*

A M Wakfer

The Lady of the House

Tonight there's a Candlelight Supper,
At the House of Bucket (Bouquet)
The cream of the county will be there -
Hyacinth's been baking all day!
(Poor Richard!)

Sheridan's proud of his Mummy,
(It's a shame that he cannot be there)
For Hyacinth knows how to do things -
A lady with true savoir faire!
('It's the breeding')

The table is laid to perfection -
('The silver's Georgian you know')
And the china is finest Crown Derby,
('So nice in the candlelight's glow')
('Tasteful, don't you think?')

Hyacinth's invited the Vicar,
The Chief of Police and the Mayor,
Also dear Dame Barbara Cartland
('To exclude her would be so unfair')
('Oh, dear me, yes!')

Emmett will play the piano,
('Background music is such an 'in' thing')
And, after the coffee and liqueurs,
Hyacinth's intending to sing!
(What a privilege!)

But, for now, Hyacinth waits in the doorway,
Assuming an elegant pose,
As three people arrive, (*uninvited!*)
It's Daisy, and Onslow, and Rose!
(Poor Hyacinth!)

Ann Bissett

Hyacinth Bucket (Pronounced Bouquet)

'Sit anywhere you like, dear.
Not there, dear, that's my chair.
Do mind the table edge, dear.
Yes, anywhere but there.

My best bone china service.
I can't get any more.
A breaker or a cup, dear?
Would you like me to pour?

Be careful with your crumbs, dear.
Don't drop them on the floor.
Oh, do you have to go, dear?
Don't you want any more?

There's Emmet! I must sing, dear.
I want the leading part.
Why is he hiding there, dear?
I'm just about to start.

Ah, Richard, wipe your feet dear.
Leave your shoes at the door.
Oh, Sheridan just called, dear.
Yes, he would like some more.

He's always short of cash, dear.
The others have so much.
He must have silk pyjamas.
They're so smooth to the touch.

There's Onslow at the door, dear,
And Rose and Daisy too.
Quick, let them in and hide them.
Before they're seen, please do.'

Joyce M Turner

Birds of a Feather - Tracey

Dorien and you, have a good time.
While Sharon is too good, or this would not rhyme.
The husbands are demons,
But true to life I agree.
Your feelings are best,
Though you keep them up your sleeve.
Your, a laugh to me,
I wait for your lines,
Whatever else is on
Your still a pleasure to see,
Don't change your ways,
It's you that makes the play,
So please make a new series,
And make my day.

M Green

To Nora Batty

Curlers form a halo
Thy lovely hair to frame
And tho' tha' often scowl at me
I love thee just the same

Thy figure, cased in whalebone,
Makes me wild with hot desire;
And a glimpse of wrinkly stockings
Sets my aching heart on fire.

Many things I'd love to say
And whisper in thy ear,
But all my dreams come out to nowt
I'm crying in my beer!

Have pity on me, Nora!
For I've loved thee hard and long,
And I want thee to come home to,
That's the burden of my song.

Sure, tha' don't like ferrets,
Or even my two friends,
And as for Compo drinking beer -
Well, can't we make amends?

For I do love thee, Nora,
From the bottom of my heart -
What's this? . . . A little smile from her?
Ee, lad! Compo's made a start!

S J Short

A Life in Black and White

This lady comes from Liverpool and was christened Priscilla White.
In the *sixties* we played her records at the Youth Club, Tuesday
night.
She used to sing at the Cavern and met Lennon and McCartney,
who
Wrote *Love of the Loved*, one of her hits and also, *It's for you.*
Her boyfriend's name was Bobby, 'You're my world', to him she said,
They've not *lost that loving feeling* in the years since they were wed.
He managed her career while they raised a family,
Then she later changed direction when she went into TV.
Being down to earth and friendly, she gets on with people great
And she used her natural talents as the hostess of *Blind Date.*
Her next move was to host a show with folks from far and near,
'Surprise, surprise', she greets them with, 'Hello, it's Cilla 'ere!'

I'm sure by now chuck, you have guessed just who has got the knack
Of making people gobsmacked, of course, it's Cilla Black.

Patricia Scott

Mrs Bucket

Polishing shelves and cleaning the house.
trying to be a tender loving spouse,
to her husband Richard, poor Dick alas,
drinking wine from plastic 'cause he's not allowed a glass.
While eating his breakfast she takes his toast,
and when the phone rings she will begin to boast.
'Oh the sister in Spain, the one with the pool',
or 'the one in America who's frightfully cool.'
Of course her friends they don't believe her,
they just don't like to say,
they get invited to candlelight suppers, but they'd rather stay away.
Oh! of course I forgot Sheridan who's as gay as a lark,
with his silk pyjamas and he's as bright as a spark.
As far as family goes she doesn't like to say,
and she makes up lies to keep them away.
When they come to pick her up they drive round again and again,
so she doesn't get seen in their car
for she has a reputation to maintain.
So if you see a lady who's full of pride today,
you can almost guarantee it's Mrs Bucket. Oh sorry Bouquet!

Elizabeth Ball

The Queen of Social Climbing

Hyacinth:
The sort of person many of us know,
every detail of her life has to be just so.
The silver must be polished in case the Vicar comes to tea
and crumpet crumbs must never be allowed to fall upon one's knee!
Her candlelight suppers are a treat for the elite.
They talk in gracious tones about Epsom and the Derby,
the hat they wore at Ascot, the cruise to the Azores,
as in blissful oblivion husband Richard snores!
Whilst Hyacinth's mind is fully awake,
lapping up each cultural comment with greedy intensity.
Longing to be a part of this frivolous social whirl,
deep down, knowing she's pretending - just like a little girl.

Leonie Cheetham

Auntie

There's lots of programmes on TV
From America's *Cheers* to *Did you See*
There's comedy, and *Question Time*
Do you remember *What's My Line*
There's films old, and some that's new
And lots of sport for us to view
Coronation Street is good
If you don't watch it, then you should
As for the kids, there's *You and Me*
And they can watch it on TV
Bob's full house is on the box
Also Opportunity Knocks
But best of all is Cilla Black
She has what other presenters lack
Her Surprise, Surprise will touch your heart
And bring together those apart.
Blind Date, well that can be such fun
And lead to Wedding Bells for some.
And Cilla's hat was rather fetching
At a *Blind Date* wedding, we were watching.
As a personality she's the tops
And hasn't she got a lot of *frocks*
Her *Bobby* gets a mention too.
And we know what her kids do.
Yes she's my favourite star of all
So if she ever makes a call
Be ready with a cup of cheer (tea)
And always say, 'I'm glad your here'
Each series is a joy to see
And we can watch it on TV.

N Ingham

Liverpool Lass

Liverpool lass with your cheeky grin,
People admire you through thick and thin,
A chirpy laugh, an open heart,
Hitting it off right from the start.

Surprise, Surprise Cilla does say,
All the years fade away,
For lonely souls with loved ones lost,
Cilla finds them and blow the cost,
Tears of joy, smiles and laughter,
She will provide the happy ever after.

Don't forget Blind Date as well,
Where many a cupid's arrow has fell,
Couples looking for love and kisses,
Cilla tries to grant their wishes,
So Liverpool lass we hold you most dear,
For brightening our lives with sunshine and cheer.

S E Windridge

Thora Hird

On Sunday when Thora announces 'Praise Be'
It's time to sit down and watch TV
Where 'ere she walks and to whom she talks
The interest she takes is so keen
That when it's time for the cameras to roll
With a sweet smile on her face she steals the show.

Now her charming ways dispel stress and strain
And in a voice that's slow and clear
For the elderly and infirm to hear,
She chats away as if to say:
Come dear friends, join in with our songs
And raise your voice Praise Be to soar
That Angels in Heaven may echo it more.

But now the scene is changed and laughter stalks to the fore
As Thora halts her dearest man, outside the kitchen door
Whilst she strews the *Daily News* along the kitchen floor
That all may be so sparkling clean
Should friends from *The Last of the Summer Wine* drop in.
Enjoying a *Cuppa* with her friends was a social dream,
And the best china came out for an airing it seems.

Now Thora took her friends for a spin in her car, passing time to fill
Tho' few nasty jerks at start, yet full of confidence still
She stepped on the pedal and stormed up the hill
Where a barrel rolling display was the highlight of the day.
So they stopped, and watched, as the game got under way
But the barrels gained speed, and the riders had a rough time indeed.

Emerging from the barrels so haggard and pale
To the pub they retired for a glass of Brown Ale.

Margaret Elsie Long

Lynda Brown - the Cook's Kitchen Garden

Lynda Brown, is quite a gal
Everybody's gardening pal
With rakish cap, and saucy grin
She keeps the crops a-rolling in.

Lots of spuds from tiny rows
Leeks and carrots too, she grows
Herbs and mustard, salad crops
Chinese greens, and turnip tops

Spinach beet, and cauliflowers
Six-foot peas can now be ours
These bygone plants of long-ago
She gives us all, the urge to grow.

This little lass gives cooking tips
That really make you smack your lips
Spinach pate, gourmet fries,
Nettle pancakes, rhubarb pies.

Parsnips baked with marmalade
Even pesto can be made
By using basil that you've grown
On window-sills inside your home

Gardening faces come and go
But even Gardeners' World must know
How much we like this fair-haired cook
Let's hope she writes a gardening book.

A A Moody

Cilla Black

She used to be a singer
And produced many a track
But she didn't become famous
'Til she changed from White to Black
Now she's on the telly
Hostess of her own shows
With husband Bobby by her side
Her fame just grows and grows
Her programme *Blind Date* is a scream
Both old and young apply
And if they meet a perfect match
Then they are home and dry
They're sent away on holiday
Maybe Whitley Bay or France
Then come back to tell us
If they found a true romance
Then 'It's Cilla here' we hear her cry
When she appears upon our screen
'It's really me chook, Surprise Surprise'
'I'll fulfil your wildest dream'
She helps folks meet their favourite stars
And long lost relations from afar
She doesn't put on airs and graces
She really is a star
She tells us tales about *our Jack*
And then she has a chortle
Once when someone admired her nice red hair
She replied 'I get it out a bottle'.

Margaret Bell

Such is Life

Con me? Never, no!
I know where most people go,
If you are caught in this trap
Let Esther's team make them snap.
Bogus salesmen, a motley crew
She'll give advice on what to do.
It's good to know, that help's at hand
With Esther and her happy gang,
If you're unsure in any way
She helps to keep those crooks at bay,
Helping with any strife,
Ah well, that's life.

Sandra Hitchens

Your Host: Miss Cilla Black

Gorgeous to look at;
Delightful to know;
Pure as a lily;
White as drift snow;
Entertainment for all;
Just by a cheery
Telephone call;

Humble; poor; deprived;
It matters not;
Searching for loved ones;
Long ago lost;

Nothing is too much trouble;
Or too great a task;
For the one and only;
Liverpool Lass;

TV shows, are top of the pops;
Miss Cilla Black is the best of the lot.

Ethel Beattie

In Praise of Anneka

Some TV girls are very nice
But none so sweet as Annie Rice!
Cool and calm is Anneka,
No situations panic her.

However hard the tasks she's set -
Like jumping from a speeding jet -
She keeps her head (and never cares)
when all around are losing theirs.

She's not afraid of any stunt -
Do you remember Treasure Hunt?
To see her running (from behind)
A nicer rear you'd never find.

To see her tossing back her hair
You'd think she never had a care.
No matter how obscure the clues
She hardly ever seemed to lose.

She looked so calm and yet so clever
When climbing steeples or whatever,
With seconds left and nothing more
She'd find what she was looking for.

Dear Anneka! Those were the days,
And now we've got this *Passport* craze,
But when she climbs up pyramids
I'm worrying in case she skids.

I liked her too in pantomime
When she played Jack one Christmastime.
I'll say she's nice with that great grin,
She'll always be my heroine.

L W Cottage

Our Esther Rantzen

The person I would choose, one of the best on TV
It's our Esther Rantzen, the woman for me,
She does so much good and helps folks in distress,
Helping to get their lives out of a mess.

One of the things in life she did choose
Was to help poor young kids fight abuse,
With her care and concern their lives can be good,
She tries to make their lives be as it really should.

Esther helps the sick, she helps the poor,
Is there anyone you know that could do more,
A hospital abroad, no medicines, they die every day,
Through her programme, two loaded trucks on their way.

She is like a fairy Godmother making dreams come true,
Children needing transplant operations, she will help them too,
Esther loves to laugh a lot, but she must shed many tears,
Helping all those people to cope with all their fears.

Life without our Esther would be so very sad,
She is one of the greatest women that we have every had,
Without her love for mankind, what would we all do?
Esther Rantzen I give the biggest Gold heart to you.

Pauline Xena

It's our Cilla

'Surprise! Surprise!' our Cilla says
On her Sunday evening show,
As she chats away to her audience,
As she moves from row to row.
She seems to know all their names,
The look of shock unreal,
For she finds both friends and family
On a show that makes you feel.
With Cilla, Bob and all her crew,
Those missing links are found,
When very little facts are known,
They dig and search around.
So if you're missing someone
And you no longer have the time,
Give details of who? when? and where?
On Cilla's phone hot line.

Kevin Bassett

Treasure Anneka

A lovely smile, and very fit,
From any challenge she won't quit!
Her style and personality
Make her a winning certainty.
Her outfits chosen are just right,
They're sporty, casual and bright.

She's friendly, clever, full of fun,
And when it's raining, she's the sun.
Her sense of humour guides her through
A *Treasure Hunt* and *Passport* too.
She's sharp and witty, and no fool,
If there's a problem, she stays cool.

Around the world she's travelled far,
In helicopter, plane and car,
Her buggy and her lorry too
Are recognised in Wedgwood blue.
So many friends and journeys made,
Plans fulfilled, foundations laid.

She also has a tender heart,
To Romania she did depart,
And with her team of helpers there,
By practical and loving care,
The orphanage was filled with joy
With clothes and toys for girl and boy.

This golden girl deserves the best,
She's passed each hard and gruelling test.
Champagne and roses all the way
Dear Anneka you make our day -
Love and laughter in good measure,
To the nation's cherished treasure!

Anne Garrett

Ladies and Gentlemen it's Miss Cilla Black

Her mam never thought when Cilla was born in Liverpool
That as queen of prime time TV she would rule.
Well, Mrs White, surprise surprise,
Your Cilla is Cinderella in disguise.
She must have had a lorra lorra luck
To become such a well known star, chuck.
From humble beginnings, singing at the start
Songs like *Anyone who had a heart*,
To TV hostess and presenter who's top rate
Was it luck that got her *Blind Date*?
Or, did she really have a fairy Godmother?
A latter day fairytale, I know no other.
Come on Cilla, it's time for confession
How to star in your profession.
So come on our Cilla, chuck
Is it really just a lorra luck?

J Carlsen

Cilla Black

I have wrote many poems fifty at best
But I feel inside this is different to the rest
I am writing this poem just for you
To show you knowledge of a TV personality and what they do,
She cares, she's kind, she's full of life
Yes! it's Cilla Black she'll release all your strife
If you watch her show then you'll know what I mean
All the tears and laughter people have seen
You've seen her charm, her kindness at heart
But her personality is the best part
The times I've laughed the way she makes you feel
The love in her heart it's one hundred per cent real
Thank you for your show, what would we do
If on a Sunday night we never had you
Our nights would be lonely. The help would be none
And without Cilla's smile we'd have no fun.
Surprise galore is what you shall get
If you watch Surprise Surprise on your TV set
So thank you Cilla for your caring heart
I always sit close when your show is to start
Cilla is from Liverpool a tremendous suburb
Keep on with your show as it's grandly superb.

Amanda Williams

Anneka Rice

There is a personality called Anneka Rice
Who will do almost anything for a price,
Her most famous feature is her bum
As it's very big to some.

She likes to do treasure hunts
And maybe pull a few stunts,
While clues she searches everywhere for
The studio keeps the score.

If you dare to *Challenge Anneka*
You can guarantee not to panic her,
As every challenge is always done
With lots of help from everyone.

So there you are she's a girl and a half
And always ready for a laugh,
So if you ever need some fun
Anneka's the one to call upon.

J Dawe

Queen of Suburbia

She rules her home and husband too
with a firm, determined mind.
A speck of dust in her tidy room
would be certainly hard to find.

She loves her sisters and Daddy too
but preferably from afar.
She visits them sometimes - when she must
in her spotless, shiny car.

People avoid her whenever they can
her bragging is widely known.
Her candlelight suppers just can't be missed
if you value a life of your own.

She offers her services all around
sure that what she does is the best.
No one refuses - they wouldn't dare,
so they're sorely put to the test.

She's Hyacinth Bucket - pronounced Bouquet
this woman so widely known.
The elegant terror of everyone's lives
as our TV has shown.

Pamela Oliver

Mrs Bucket

She's Hyacinth Bucket pronounced the French way,
Dreaded by neighbours but here to stay!
With china, Elizabeth is all fingers and thumbs,
Feeling uneasy and avoiding the crumbs.
Her musical soirees make the vicar despair,
He devises excuses why he cannot be there.
Those candlelight dinners to impress the chosen few,
Are something to remember with her *Perriwinkle* too.
Her son Sheridan is her pride and joy
Whose degree is amazing and a real mummy's boy!
Of all her sisters, only Violet makes her proud,
And boasts of her swimming pool and Mercedes to a crowd.
But Onslow and Rose make her shudder with shame
How can they disgrace the fine family name?
With eye-raising short skirts
- Such undignified show,
And not wearing a suit and tie
Is an offence - don't you know?
That diabolical car, with its engine of smoke
Is unsightly and crude and their house is a joke.
Well, it's all very well if they stay in their space
And not associate near Hyacinth's place.
For creating a good impression is the name of the game,
And her residence is proof that her life is the same.
. . . Oh! Richard, dear Richard, don't you ever mind?
Obedient and faithful and forever resigned.
Don't you ever wish that you could rebel?
And there's just one person that you could tell.
And unburden your soul and have your say,
But you'd probably tell the whole world you *love* Mrs Bucket!

Felicia Isaacs

Ode to Diana

The lovely Diana,
She really loves Tom,
In television's favourite
Weekly sitcom.
She fights and she argues,
(They never agree!)
But theirs is a love
So easy to see.
Please Tom, pop the question
To Diana, and soon.
And can I come with you,
On your honeymoon?

E Collinson

Untitled

Her auburn hair's from a bottle
A surgeon has fashioned her nose,
She changed her name to bring her fame
And wears designer clothes.

She's a star - there is no question
This lass from Liverpool,
She learned to sing and entertain
Before she went to school.

She brings a lorra lorra laughs
Surprises by the dozen,
Sister meeting brother again
Or maybe a long lost cousin.

The handsome lads and pretty girls
Don't always get along,
Blind dates can be disaster
When Cilla gets it wrong.

You're my World she sang
And topped the charts,
In the all too distant past
The song is gone - but Cilla goes on
This girl was built to last.

We watch you on the telly
And know what a star you are,
The girl next door made the big time
With a smile and a wave *Ta rah!*

P Sampson

What a Bird our Neighbour is

Dark hair, dark eyes, quite petite
Vivacious, sultry, and sometimes sweet
Miniskirt high heeled shoes
From all the men she can choose.

She is the type of woman
That the men fall for,
But to us who live next door
She's really quite a bore.

Quite unannounced she will pop in
Says wherever have you been,
Been ringing you for a long long time
Oh! by the way, this is Brian.

Tall and blonde with a gorgeous tan
There he stands this hunk of man,
Just picked him up she says casually
From a kiss-a-gram.

She's quite a snob
But she can be,
Kind and full of sympathy
For all she is, we still like Dorien.

H Turvill

Waiting for God

Diane sits and quietly waits
While Tom goes off again
Today he's fighting for his life
In the civil war of Spain.
What is age? she asks herself
Does it really matter.
Everybody will grow old
Getting grey and fatter.
I go upstairs and wonder why.
My legs are weak and trembly
What happened to your sturdy knees
You thought would play at Wembley?
It is what you feel inside
Not how you look to others
They would never understand
You still can dream of lovers.
We cannot hurry quite so much
You certainly are slower
And with the best will in the world
You cannot push the mower.
But how nice to have the time
To visit and to talk,
To watch the telly, read a book
Or take a gentle walk.
The clock ticks slowly on and on
So treasure every day
For when He calls 'your time is up'
You know you cannot stay.

E M Clowes

Hyacinth Bucket

The telephone rings out in the hall,
It's answered straight away,
'The Lady of the house speaking'
It's Hyacinth Bucket.

'Oh do be quiet Richard'
I can't hear a word they say
I tell you it's not Bucket
But Bookay I said Bookay.

A message from our Daisy
She wants to visit me
She'd better wait until it's dark
In case the neighbours see.

She's bound to bring her Onslo,
With his vest all full of holes.
He never wears a shirt or tie,
And always on the dole.

She can bring my other sister
The one that's known as Rose,
But leave behind our Violet
'Cos her man wears women's clothes.

My son? YesSheridan is very well
He is my pride and joy.
But I'm afraid he will stay single
While he's with that Tarquin boy.

And now the door bell's ringing
My goodness! Oh dear me,
It's daddy with his girlfriend
And the Vicar's due for tea.

S Atyeo

Keeping Up Appearances

'Not Bucket - Bouquet,
It's pronounced that way,
Please do try to remember that dear.'

'For I'm afraid that tonight,
If you can't get it right,
You'll be eating elsewhere I fear.'

'For my candlelight suppers are second to none,
Everyone comes who's anyone,
I've invited a Lord and a Dame.'

'But I won't entertain,
When the china is lain,
One who cannot pronounce my own name.'

'So remember this Richard my dear,
Pronounce the name loudly and clear,
And if you dress smart,
And play well your part,
I'll introduce you as my husband this year.'

Janette Austin

Untitled

Delia Smith's the girl for me
Wonderful cakes and buns for tea,
Tries to teach me to do the same
But they never turn out the same again.

J G Button

Anne Diamond and Nick Owen

This woman I see on TV
Is one heck of a gutsy lady,
She's been through the mill, both well and ill
And always bounced back daily.

She's been on early TV
She's even been on late,
But now she's on in the morning
It gives me time to be awake.

Anne Diamond has campaigned
For important issues to be portrayed,
Plenty of women quite like me
Have turned around and said, 'did you see.'

I watch Anne each morning with Nick
And get most annoyed if I go out and miss,
The TV twosome that portray
The way I would like to relax and stay.

I watched their careers through the years
Their ups and downs and their fears,
I admire their courage and their strength
It gives me pleasure to see them content.

May their futures be good and kind
As I watch them both full of pride,
The TV twosome I sit with empty mind
I relax and think of the sands and tide.

They educate me and others alike
They twiddled their toes to my delight,
They're not stuck up like some we see
That I know others will agree.

All I'm left to say is, is there any job left
There for me. I can't tell you how happy I'd be.

A Brimfield

Quiche Lorraine

I wake up in the morning
I turn the TV on
And there she is our own Lorraine
Looking fresh as early dawn
She's always cheery, laughing
But solemn when required
The powers that be at ITV
Were wise when she they hired
Her accent is so charming
Her nature quite unique
With wisdom, great intelligence
And a dash of tongue in cheek.
An appetising recipe
To whet the appetite
And when you've had a sample
Quiche Lorraine Kelly!
Is just right!
So here's to you
Our own Lorraine
I salute you with a half
And may you long continue
To give us all a laugh!

Mary Morton

Judy Meacock

She comes in my house most evenings
With a beautiful face and a smile,
She cocks her head as to Bob she says
It's your turn now! boy she's got style.
I miss her at the weekend
The news becomes a bore,
Because Lucy's not there to read it
So I just sit back and snore,
There's no one on the show quite like her
She's pretty and she's sweet,
She's quick to make a smart retort
That could knock you off your feet
Now if you have not seen her
May I suggest you do,
I'm sure you will enjoy her
As much as I do too.
I'm sure you will recognise her
She is the smile with the fringe on top,
And ask me what her name is
Why it's Judy Meacock.

M Kay

Anne Diamond

Anne Diamond a lady of charm
So now happily has a new bairn,
Watching her on TV every day
We hope she always will stay.
Her wonderful help on babies cot deaths
Has brought down the sorrow many felt,
I only wish I had a say
I'd give her a medal any day.

I M Townsend

Headline

The perfect presenter of world events,
Without a hint of impertinence.
Moira Stuart, holds me in her spell.
Once, that beautiful, tight, top lip fell
Into a permitted smile. (re/ cricket match.)
What a catch, brown eyes twinkled,
brown nose wrinkled, straight eyebrow crinkled.
Into a permitted smile?

Jean Wythe

Obsession

Of all the stars seen on TV,
There's one who means so much to me.
I think she is completely lovely -
You've got it - Yes! - Joanna Lumley!

Enticing and so very tempting,
She surely does send men's hearts rending!
And oh! - Her Muller's Ad -
The best PR they've ever had!

She *sells* the product - so exciting!
Her vamping skills are quite enticing!
She's always cultured - excudes charm,
There's really no-one she would harm.

And on TV - what a *production!*
It's just all glorious seduction!
She plays the part of temptress well -
Soon Shakespeare? - Only time will tell.

Genteel, refined - so softly spoken -
How many hearts must she have broken?
But in conclusion - can I say -
'Joanna - please come out to play!'

Ian Simpson

Kate Adie

That of all women you should do me honour,
Come with such worship to my servant door;
Its hearth glows, like a bride serene and tender:
The voyager embarks on his own floor.

When first you crossed this threshold, as a stranger,
One of the motley crowds that throng the street,
Rude wonder dared incredulous devotion. . .
I had no mention of a form so sweet.

Sleep counselled dreams to publish their perfection,
Hope, too, conspired your image to proclaim;
Dew-petalled dawns grew pensive with reflection,
From fluted bird-song morning sought a name.

Still reeled the chaliced sun in drunken splendour,
Occasioning each dusk-spill accident;
The world revolved an ordinary glory,
Unrumourous and silent of portent.

Yet now, above the crystalled silver leaning
You trim the tapers at our dining board,
Your wifery a ruby, rich revealing
The home mere habitation disaffords.

Whilst since you sit, with folded grance and simple,
Grey evening threads ablent on day's bright loom,
Firelight and shadow glinting from quiet's thimble -
O, woman beautiful with passion's bloom.

I shall not custom this possession nightly,
Nor crush your spirit in too fierce embrace:
Enough, at twilit hour, from toil returning,
Beside, close-leaned, to laud your lovelier face.

Beth Beckenham

Cilla Black

Surprise Surprise it's Cilla here
With her accent oh so queer.
More of a shock than a surprise,
Producing lost relatives before your eyes.

Blind Dates another unusual sight,
Three choices to make, and they can't get it right.
The destination choice is also a shock,
A day out in Luton, instead of Bangkok.

Oh! no is Cilla going to sing?
In the sixties she was all the thing,
But in these days of Pop and Rap,
For God's sake Cilla shut your trap.

Now dear old Bobby gets a mention,
Leaves me in a state of tension.
Then on and on about our Jack,
This really gets right up my back.

She's on the box day after day
I just can't seem to get away.
There she is when I switch on
I'll wait a while and hope she's gone.

Perhaps my comments seem over zealous,
In point of fact I'm only jealous.
The same age as me and she looks great,
When I'm well past my sell-by date.

Still with her money and her clothes
I could strike a better pose.
Surprise Surprise I like her though,
And I would never miss her show.

Sylvia Cooper

Lovely Joanna

She's absolutely fabulous in many different ways,
With model looks and model voice,
No matter the part she plays.
As a drunkard she was super,
As an Avenger she was great,
Even eating those Fruit Corners,
Does she *never* put on weight?

Low and sexy is her voice,
She has taste and style.
And she accompanies her every line,
With that naughty smile.

We think Joanna's smashing,
Her looks have stately purity,
She guided us thro' our early fashion,
Now she'll lead us in our maturity.

Wyn Mary Martin

Cilla's Surprise

What a wonderful programme is Surprise Surprise
When long lost relatives appear before your eyes,
How very happy Cilla and Co must be
When love is revived for all to see.
Some stories are tragic and some are sad
But oh! what a pleasure to make someone glad.
After the parting of years and years to remember
The times when love was so dear and so tender.
And to share the joy for everyone to see
What more can you say it's all on TV,
You get violence and sex and drugs and abuse
And lots of bad language not a lot of use.
I take my hat off to Cilla and company
In the same situation they'd do for me,
As they've done for others not so lucky as I
My family's around me, I've no need to cry.
What a comfort it must be to give so much pleasure
To people so grateful and forever will treasure,
The wonderful memories of that fabulous night
How good they must feel when things turn out right.

Joan Evans

Morning Star

The wee cute Scottish girl
The queen of breakfast telly.
The one and only morning belle
The lovely Lorraine Kelly.
Brightening up the morning blues
With a smile so sparkling bright,
A special touch to the news
She's really out of sight.
With twinkling eyes framed in glass
For all the world to see,
Making the show a higher class
For good old GMTV..
Handling items with such a grace
With feeling and good taste,
Putting bullies in their place
To loose her would be a waste.
No one comes close to the lovely Lorraine
A woman who's bound to go far,
She chases away the grey and the rain
Our wonderful morning star.

Alan Denne

My Lovely Lorraine

Forgive, the sadness, of this refrain
Though, we've never met, I sense your pain

With my heart filled with much regret
We will never meet, we have not yet

Oh, my sweet, lovely, Lorraine
My tears fall, just like the rain

You possess a beautiful warm smile
But, alas, my aimless life seems futile

I admire your warm Scottish accent
The world full of sorrow, fills me with dissent

If never, just to gaze upon your eyes
T'would be for me, a great surprise

Alas, I only see you on the television
For me you are a magical vision

Forgive this poet, his simple dream
For his tears run, like the stream

Think of me, I pray, not unkind
For it matter not, of me I don't mind

Once more, it seems, I wait for the telly
Once more to see, lovely *Lorraine Kelly*.

J Felton

That's Life

'Hi there, I'm Esther, would you mind telling me
Exactly what you like to watch on TV.'
'Oh I love the sports and the Saturday reports,
And the commentary on BBC.'

'And you there, Sir, a moment if you will.'
'Well, I like the dramas like Morse and the Bill,
And to watch a good thriller, and guess who's the killer
And James Bond - like that View to a Kill.'

'What about your wife, come here now don't hide.'
'Me! I'm fond of Coronation Street and soaps like Brookside
But I really must scoff, since they took Crossroads off
That it's just not the same - though they've tried.'

'Let's ask over here . . . we're discussing TV.'
'Eeh . . . there's *nowt* any better than a good comedy
And the best altogether is Birds of a Feather
And that *In Sickness and Health* tickled me !'

'Shall we ask this young boy here, hey, that's a smart hat
What's good on the telly?' 'Oh . . . um . . . er . . . Postman Pat!'
'Do you like Jackanory, when they tell you a story'
'No but I do like Garfield the Cat!'

'Well, as you have seen there are so many views
with so many programmes, it's no problem to choose
. . . Please Officer . . . if we can . . . I won't go in the van
Do you always arrest TV crews?'

L Barrasford